RISE & THRIVE:

Quotes To Start Your Day

For A Positive Mindset

Lisa Blackshaw

Dedication

I dedicate this book to the birds
who want to catch the early worm.

"We become the
books we read. »

~ Matthew Kelly

Epigraph

"Positive"

ADJECTIVE
*If you are positive about things,
you are hopeful and confident,
and think of the good aspects of a situation
rather than the bad ones.*

ADJECTIVE
*If you make a positive decision or
take positive action, you do something definite
to deal with a task or problem.*

ADJECTIVE
*If you are positive about something,
you are completely sure about it.*

"Rise"

VERB
When you rise, you get out of bed.

VERB
If an emotion rises in someone,
they feel it suddenly,
so intensely it affects their behaviour.

SINGULAR NOUN
The rise of someone is the process by which they
become more important, successful, or powerful.

COUNTABLE NOUN
A rise in the amount of something is an increase in it.

"Thrive"

VERB
*If someone or something thrives,
they do well and are successful,
healthy or strong.*

VERB
*To grow vigorously or luxuriantly;
improve physically.*

Contents

Rise & Thrive is about waking each day with a positive attitude, armed with a structure to guide you through each morning, empowering your decision-making throughout your life. It is an ethos to live by. Early rising brings success depending on what you DO with your time once you're up. An accomplished life is derived from a positive start in the morning and repeating it every day to consistently excel and see the results you desire.

" Morning is an important time of day, because how you spend your morning can often tell you what kind of day you are going to have.. "

~ Lemony Snicket

A good quote serves many purposes and the use of motivational ones when you first wake up can set your mind on the right path for the day. Quotes help us put our own opinions and emotions into perspective, allowing us to channel the words of others or to interpret a message from within.

We experience a sense of harmony when we find our feelings, experiences, and observations match those of another. That thought, 'hey, I feel like that too!' can make us a bit more in tune and at ease with the world and a little less lonely.

> **"Quotes and write-ups are just theoretical consolation, what we really need to do is practically apply them."**
>
> **~ Sara Arif**

Morning

"*Few ever lived to old age,*
and fewer still ever became distinguished,
who were not in the habit of early rising."

~ John Todd

Tell yourself – NOW – that improving your life is attainable by setting up a morning routine built for success.

If you Google 'good morning schedule', you will find plenty of advice on how to enhance your day. Results will look something like this:

- **Drink water**
- **Eat breakfast**
- **Make your bed**
- **Journal**
- **Exercise**
- **Meditate**

After researching morning schedules, you will find reading is one of the best things you can do to activate your brain. This is where *Rise & Thrive*: For A Positive Mindset comes in. Reading this book can be one of the building blocks in your morning program.

"No one ever taught us that by
learning how to consciously set our intention
to wake up each morning with a genuine
desire—even enthusiam—to do so,
we can change our entire lives."

~ Hal Elrod

"An ordinary life is all about daily,
continuous improvements in the
areas that matter most."

~ Robin Sharma

You may work shifts, have a disability, be retired, be a parent, be a student, be a caregiver, or have another personal circumstance which requires you to adjust your morning schedule to meet your needs. *Rise & Thrive* is going to encourage you to make positive changes in your routine.

"Let us make our future now, and let us make our dreams tomorrow's reality. **"**

Malala Yousafzai

" Be patient with yourself.
Self-growth is tender;
it's holy ground.
There's no greater investment. „

~ Stephen Covey

Spiritual, intellectual, emotional, familial, physical or financial development... whichever area you seek to make progress, this book aims to guide and inspire your direction.

The morning is the best time to set your goals and line up your day to achieve them. It's not enough to speak your goals and just expect results. You need to make the time and put in the effort required to reach them. Utilise your morning like all successful people do.

Positive Thinking

"It does not matter how long
you are spending on the earth,
how much money you have gathered
or how much attention you have received.
It is the amount of positive vibration
you have radiated in life that matters. "

~ Amit Ray

When we wake up in the morning, we need to find some positive energy to make the day a success. We're going to create this energy by controlling our first thoughts to hum an optimistic tune! Positivity is a choice and when you choose it, you will quickly feel the rewards in all aspects of your health. Staying positive takes practice, so let's run through the tactics used to gain a positive mindset and discover their benefits!

A positive attitude can increase your lifespan by 11-15%. By actively thinking more positive thoughts you are more likely to reach the age of 85 and beyond! Don't dread getting older, embrace it, and look forward to your future years. In turn, this determines your will to live and you actively preserve your general health and well-being. This approach is a domino effect of positive results.

Positive thinkers generally have lower rates of depression and less stress, which reduces the likelihood of chronic diseases. This zen way of living improves your immune system so that your resistance is stronger against bugs, like the common cold. These findings have not been backed up with medical research just yet, but the evidence suggests that the mind has some power over the immune system.

> **"When we are ready to make positive changes in our lives, we attract whatever we need to help us."**
>
> **~ Louise Hay**

"Life changes very quickly,
in a very positive way, if you let it."

~ Lindsey Vonn

"The day she let go of the things that
were weighing her down, was the day
she began to shine the brightest."

~ Katrina Mayer

Don't fill your environment with negative pictures and negative talk because your belief system will shift in that direction. It all starts with believing that you can... then you will. Your mind is a factory churning out thoughts, and those thoughts become your actions and guide you towards your goals. Don't just think positively, speak positively too. This way, you will receive more uplifting feedback and start a cycle of positivism.

" Every person takes the limit of their own field of vision for the limits of the world. "

~ Arthur Schopenhauer

Happiness is associated with regular positive thinking. Focus on the good in most situations. Negative thoughts make us paranoid, on edge, worried, and anxious. These emotions are not relaxing. You can't be positive all the time, as there are occasions where you need to be pragmatic. Don't ignore reality, but don't let your mind wander down that dyslogistic and pessimistic rabbit hole which can lead to hopelessness and feelings of defeat. Overcoming adversity and feeling gratitude yields happiness.

> **" The flower that blooms in adversity is the most rare and beautiful of all. "**
>
> **~ Mulan**

Be aware of your thoughts and recognise the entrance to that rabbit hole to avoid the downward spiral, look for the silver lining.

" Thus, a wise individual is the one who learns to see positive even in unfavorable events and unanticipated behaviour of people. "

~ Lindsay J. Hallie

You can achieve financial success from thinking positively. Create a plan to improve your finances and spend a few moments in the morning deciding how your day is going to align with this strategy. Eliminate bad debt, increase your saving habits, reduce your spending habits and research new investments. Depending on how high you set your financial goals, unfortunately, they don't transpire overnight. Just getting out of debt and back in the red can take some time. Your plan might include how to get that promotion you've had your eye on. Regardless of your intentions, pursue them all with a positive mental attitude and the law of attraction will deliver in abundance.

" Inspiration comes from within yourself. One has to be positive. When you're positive, good things happen. "

~ Deep Roy

> **"** The positive thinker sees the invisible,
> feels the intangible, and achieves the impossible. **"**
>
> **~ Winston Churchill**

Positive thinking is the way to live! It can create real value in your life and help you develop a greater appreciation for everything in it.

So how does one think positively? You can try using affirmations which reinforce positive thoughts from the word go. Put some of *Rise & Thrive*'s most uplifting quotes on your fridge, in your journal, on your computer desktop or pin a post it note by your bed.

> **" Positive thinking will let you do
> everything better than negative thinking will. "**
>
> **~ Zig Ziglar**

" Optimism is a happiness magnet.
If you stay positive, good things and
good people will be drawn to you. "

~ Mary Lou Retton

Join the 'positive thinkers' club and recruit new members! Surrounding yourself with other positive minds is contagious and elevating. START the day on a positive note with *Rise & Thrive* and recommend your club members to do the same. Suggest a regular meeting to read through it together! Return to *Rise & Thrive* as a positivity manual later in the day if you're flaking and feel those negative thoughts are getting the better of you.

How To Utilise This Book

" Yesterday I was clever,
so I wanted to change the world.
Today I am wise, so I am
changing myself. „

~ Rumi

You've decided to give the book a try, to see if some light morning reading will steer the course of your day in a positive way – so why not give it your all?

Not all mornings start in the same way.

Is it the weekend?

Do you have an important deadline at work?

Are you attending a family occasion?

Are you feeling unproductive?

Do you need some perspective?

**Are you feeling under the weather,
but need to push on and get through the day?**

Hopefully, you're feeling energised and ready to get this show on the road.

Returning to the same quotes can act as a mantra specific to your journey of personal development. One quote can apply to multiple life situations or different moods throughout your progression. Jot down notes throughout your *Rise & Thrive* journey and save the most intriguing insights and ideas so that you can see the most valuable lessons you have learned.

Too many quotes could be overwhelming. After ten quotes, you may stop taking in the meaning of each one. So how do you eat an elephant? One bite at a time. This is your morning – you own it – do it your way! Take your time with *Rise & Thrive*. There is no rush! If you read the whole thing in a week, a month, a year or a decade… or reread it… it's your prerogative. The aim is not to 'finish' reading it but use the power of the quotes to set you on the right path for today.

Think of *Rise & Thrive* as a morning companion to reference the great thoughts of others who can guide you in different ways through life. The book isn't going to change if you read it 10 times, but YOU will change from reading it 10 times.

" we are what we repeatedly do. Excellence, then, is not an act, but a habit. **"**

~ Will Durant

Practise Gratitude

"*Acknowledging the good
that you already have in your life
is the foundation for all abundance.*"

~ Eckhart Tolle

Learn how to really take the time to notice and reflect on the small but important things and ignore frivolous noise. Find three things each day to appreciate. Nurture and cherish your relationships. Say or do something nice for a colleague, friend or family member. Watching them be happy from your actions will reflect right back. Smile more often, write thank you notes, give compliments and don't forget how lucky you are to be YOU.

Affirmations

❝ I CAN SHAKE OFF EVERYTHING AS
I WRITE; MY SORROWS DISAPPEAR,
MY COURAGE IS REBORN. **❞**

~ Anne Frank

Keep a journal and record an 'affirmation of the day'. The affirmations don't have to be different every day, but make sure they align with your mission. For example, you could pick from your favourite *Rise & Thrive* quotes to manifest positive behaviour in your actions.

Laugh

❝ I live to laugh, and I laugh to live. ❞

~ Milton Berle

Laughing at your problems won't necessarily solve them, but making others laugh is enjoyable and can make you feel good to your core. Humour can be healing and relaxing. You can practice laughter yoga (which is laughable) – but don't knock it until you try it. At first, you may feel uncomfortable, but once your belly is hurting and tears are rolling down your cheeks, you let go of your inhibitions and feel liberated. Manufactured giggles can quickly transform into the real deal.

Meditate

" The thing about meditation is:
you become more and more you. "

~ David Lynch

To start, try a guided meditation. Begin with a 5-10 minute session until you get the hang of the techniques. Simple methods like deep breathing can clear your mind to create feelings of serenity and contentment. Let go of stress and all your problems during this exercise. Once you improve your ability to meditate, you can change the subconscious layers of your mind, remove the clutter, and better control your thoughts.

Listen

"WHERE WORDS FAIL, MUSIC SPEAKS."

~ Hans Christian Andersen

There's nothing like happy music to boost your mood! Play one of your favourite songs whilst you're journaling, exercising, drinking your first cup of coffee; or during any of your morning routine activities. Listen to podcasts, TED talks, audiobooks or anything to encourage a positive mindset and inspire you for the rest of the day. Songs are synonymous with memories, so create a playlist full of music to take you back to joyful times.

Learn To Say NO

" Half the troubles of this life can be traced to saying 'yes' too quickly and not saying 'no' soon enough. "

~ Josh Billings

People can't take your energy on demand. Give yourself permission to decline others' vibes if they are going to zap your happiness. Saying no is a powerful choice and the ultimate act of self-care. Give it a try and see how much more focus, freedom, and time you have to work on your personal development. It's not easy at first, and you shouldn't start saying no to everyone all the time from now on! No doesn't necessarily show a lack of generosity so don't feel guilty. Saying no means you open yourself to saying yes to more important commitments. Don't be afraid to disappoint others - there will be a next time.

> "Self-Improvement and success go hand in hand. Taking the steps to make yourself a better and more well-rounded individual will prove to be a wise decision."
>
> ~ **Frank Long**

How will positivity make you successful? If you have a positive outlook on life, that attitude is going to give you the confidence required to achieve your goals. Repeat this to yourself, 'I can do this!' Once you get the hang of positive thinking, your approach to problems will be a breeze. It will amplify your decision-making without having the need to give up so easily.

So now you know the benefits of positive thinking and how to do it, but how are you going to keep it up? You need a routine and the consistency it provides. Find what works for you and keep on repeating it. Continue to read *Rise & Thrive* to help manifest this positive behaviour. Stay focused. Stay positive. Keep your positive thinking cap on and use it as a key to unlock your successes.

"If you want to fly, give up everything that weighs you down."

~ Gurubogsa

Negative Thinking

" Develop success from failures.
Discouragement and failure are two
of the surest stepping stones to success. **"**

~ Dale Carnegie

There are some benefits to negative thinking too, so let's take a look at the other side of the coin. You could call it the positive power of negative thinking. When negative circumstances arise, it's completely normal to experience negative thoughts, but we must learn to deal with them effectively.

" It turns out that adversity and failure are actually useful and even necessary for developing strong-minded and successful adults **"**

~ Mark Manson

> **"If you change the way you look at things, the things you look at change."**
>
> **– Dr. Wayne Dyer**

We can utilise negative thinking as a tool to motivate us. When we think of the worst-case scenario, we want to do all that we can to prevent the bad situation from happening. This puts the positive attitude into gear and the happy wheels into motion.

Negative thinking alerts us of a problem or a danger which needs attention. Our survival instincts are desperate and anxious, but the reason to survive is a happy ending! Hopefully, you are fortunate enough never to be in a position where you're living in survival mode.

Being suspicious could help you avoid scams or phishing while empowering you to save time and money. Negative thinking slows your brain down from weighing up a situation, so listen to your gut and make the right decision. Critical thinkers make fewer mistakes, are less gullible, and able to communicate better.

❝ The ability to communicate fluidly and effectively is more than just a skill that one develops over time. It is a combination of skill, and wisdom, and the ability to connect to the perception of another that will allow them to see things the way you do and follow along with your will. **❞**

~ Gerald Campbell

Use *Rise & Thrive* to keep your mental health in check. Prolonged periods of negative thoughts can lead to illness, anxiety, discouragement, fear, and stress. Positive people in your life might avoid spending time with you if that negative energy lingers longer than it should.

" Try not to become a person of success, but rather try to become a person of value. "

~ **Albert Einstein**

Learn to identify your negative feelings and differentiate between useful emotions and deprecating ones. What triggers your brain to put the dark perspective glasses on? Recognise the associations you make with this dark place and put the sunglasses back on! Don't let your vision be overcome with negative notions.

"WHAT CONSUMES YOUR MIND CONTROLS YOUR LIFE"

~ Sara Arif

Out goes the negative train and in rolls the positive train to the platform of your brain! It's not fun to be 'Negative Ned'. We especially don't want to wake up as a 'Debbie Downer'. It's a balancing act to embrace positive actions and monitor negative vibes.

" *The pessimist sees difficulty in every opportunity. The optimist sees opportunity in every difficulty.* **"**

~ Winston Churchill

Don't bury your feelings of doubt or hesitation. You also shouldn't ignore feelings of sadness or suppress your fears and lose touch with reality. Maintain a positive energy level as best as you can during the peaks and troughs of your daily activities.

" It is important to expect nothing, to take every experience, including the negative ones, as merely steps on the path, and to proceed. "

~ Ram Dass

You can't avoid the hard times in life completely, and nor should you try to, but we want to attract positivity and apply it to lead a happy and fulfilling lifestyle. If you are grieving or experiencing trauma, then ask yourself, 'what would I say to a friend who is going through the same thing?' If you are suffering from depression, make sure you seek professional help and use *Rise & Thrive* as a guide to bring you back into the light.

" Every day may not be good but there is something good in every day. "
~ Unknown

Finding Time

" Let's get up an hour early
to live an hour more. „

~ Unknown

We all wish that there were more hours in the day. It's possible, even easy, to create this time! Analyse your day and see where you're using your time poorly. How could it be better spent? We all need the evening time to relax but if your relaxation time continues until 2am and you set off to work 30 minutes after waking up… you will agree that the percentage of your 'relaxing time' is greater than your 'productive time'.

If the scales of productivity are imbalanced, then distribute your day wisely and invest more of your time in advantageous tasks to score results. Attempt going to bed an hour earlier and wake up an hour earlier to see how this works for you. Bookend your day with good routines. Your earlier wakeup call should make you feel tired sooner than usual in the evenings, and you'll quickly get into the swing of your new bedtime. Work your way slowly to increase the minutes invested into your mornings and steal time little by little from your evenings. Be more disciplined in the morning and you'll rapidly discover that you are more disciplined throughout the rest of your day.

Why Should You Read First Thing In The Morning?

" With the new day comes
new strength and new thoughts. **"**

~ Eleanor Roosevelt

The morning is the best time for you to read because it's usually the quietest time - before the rest of the house is up and about. Maybe you love books but you're just not a morning person. Mornings are not the enemy – promise! Mornings can be the BEST if you choose to be productive during this portion of the day. Building a new habit takes time to become accustomed to, but the results are worth it. Turn to your friends and family who can help hold you accountable for your new early rising habit.

" Our lives change when our habits change. "
~ Matthew Kelly

" There are times when we stop, we sit still. We listen and breezes from a whole other world begin to whisper. "
~ James Carroll

Reading has been proven to reduce stress. Our best days cannot, and will not, start off by rushing around and feeling anxious. We want to stimulate our minds when the morning breaks! According to Mindlab International at the University of Sussex, reading for just six minutes can reduce stress by 68%!

It also works better and faster than other ways to unwind, which includes listening to music, having a hot beverage, or going for a walk. Who'd have thought? The brain is most active when you first wake up, so it's more capable of storing information. This is the period when you have the most amount of energy – so use it to focus.

Reading a book creates new memories, so your brain forms new connections between neurons (called synapses) and strengthens the existing ones. As you read, you are memorising and recalling letters, words, places, ideas, names, and actions. You're exercising your brain and improving your memory. Fantastic!

" *She read books as one would breathe air, to fill up and live.* "
~ Annie Dillard

If your goal is to increase the number of books you read, then making a small change, such as reading for 15–30 minutes when you wake up, is going to massively help you achieve this. If you read for 15 minutes every single morning, you would complete around 18–23 books per year. That's the power of consistency. By improving your morning routine to incorporate reading, you create a time slot dedicated to your personal development. You may feel too tired or a lack focus while working on your personal development later in the day, or worse, after you finish work when you don't feel motivated. So, make the most of that fresh morning energy.

"The journey of a lifetime starts with the turning of a page."

~ Rachel Anders

Your morning is sacred, so even if you don't read, whatever you do, do not watch TV! Netflix should be a treat in the evenings after you've achieved your daily intentions. Use the morning time to stimulate your mind and reserve the evening for your relaxation.

" I'm always thinking about creating. My future starts when I wake up every morning. Every day I find something creative to do with my life. **"**

~ Miles Davis

When Do I Start?

"Arise, awake, stop not till the goal is reached. "

~ Swami Vivekananda

You already have! However, the first day of the week or month is usually the ideal time to start a new routine or habit. This is when we have more hope which is a motivating tool. Ask yourself, 'what do I want to gain from this book?' The answer should be easy-peasy. To rise out of bed and thrive for the rest of the day brimming full of positivity! This is setting your intention. Eyes on the prize. You want to benefit from the opportunities afforded to morning people.

Identify who you want to be when you are goal setting. That may seem extreme because you don't want a personality tranplant JUST to wake up in the morning. However, if you tell people "I'm a positive person" and identify with that, you will begin to transform into that person. This identity will motivate you.

" SET YOUR GOALS HIGH, AND DON'T STOP TILL YOU GET THERE. "

~ Bo Jackson

If you're awake before everyone else in your house, then the morning is perfect for thinking uninterrupted. If you live with early risers then they can certainly assist in helping you form this new early habit. But once you're all up, you need to create a sanctuary of your own to fulfil your morning tasks. You may not know you're living with early risers until you get up early yourself!

Explain to your partner, family, or housemates WHY you are trying this. Make them aware of the physical and mental space you need to give it a chance. You want their support to help you thrive!

"You will never change your life until you change something you do daily. The secret of success is found in your daily routine."

~ John C. Maxwell

> **❝** I can't change the direction of the wind, but I can adjust my sails to always reach my destination. **❞**
>
> **~ Jimmy Dean**

We had to adjust to a different routine in 2020 with lockdown procedures to limit the spread of COVID-19. The whole globe had to find a 'new normal'. Whether we liked it or not, we all involuntarily changed our routines, cancelled our social calendars, and implemented new habits to stay safe. Some worked from home for the first time. Our children became accustomed to home-schooling. Our hair, nails, and other pampering went without the luxury of grooming for longer than we've ever had to anticipate. How long did that take? You had this routine and the sanitising habits imposed on you and it wasn't out of choice. Take control of the habits you know are going to improve your life.

What Type Of Book Should I Read?

" Reading is a way for me to expand my mind, open my eyes, and fill up my heart. **"**

~ Oprah Winfrey

Hopefully this one! But *Rise & Thrive* won't take it personally if you choose another book!

Of course, you need to pick the right books to learn from so that you can accelerate in your selected field and personal growth. Humans thrive on knowledge and we don't want to stop learning. We recognise the power of understanding.

The power of books is in the action you take with the knowledge you have gained. Reading will broaden your horizons; so read all types of books and you may discover a new hobby or passion. Control the input you're feeding your brain.

Reading Improves
Your Communication

" Only through communication
can human life hold meaning. „

~ Paulo Freire

Because it IS a form of communication! I think all of us will admit that this is a skill which we would like to develop; whether it's with our colleagues at the office or with our family at home. Reading in the mornings will expose you to new words and theories so that your vocabulary expands and your knowledge magnifies. The more you read, the more you know, and the more you will understand. Depending on your reading list, you are naturally going to become more intellectual by reading every day and who knows where that could lead?

> **"Sometimes success is less about making good habits easy and more about making bad habits hard."**
>
> **~ James Clear**

Self Improvement Can Be Unlocked By Reading

"Make books a part of your day, and they will make happiness a part of your life. **"**

~ Unknown

By reading more, you'll be better equipped to excel in business and life. You'll be able to beat your competition. The main objective, however, should be to try and better yourself so you can smash your own goals and make your dreams a reality. Dedicating an allocated time for a book in your morning routine is an expedient way to get you in the habit of reading more. After reading for 15 minutes in the morning you might be inspired to return to your book later in the day, you might even prefer reading your book instead of watching a TV series! Anyway, you're already reading the start of this book, so you don't need convincing of reading's many benefits!

" Reading is one of the most important activities, which helps to educate genius and develop creative abilities. "

~ Samuel Greenberg

Recommendations On How To Wake Up

"*Live life to the fullest and focus on the positive.*"

~ Matt Cameron

Can you remember your dream?
Keep a dream journal for a few weeks or record a short synopsis if you already have a daily journal.

What makes you happy?
Emotions are created by thoughts, so by asking yourself this question you will naturally feel more positive.

Are you grateful?
Reflect and list five things you are grateful for at the end of the day and leave it next to your bed, then read them when you first wake up. Gratitude is so important and will really brighten up your day.

Are you feeling relaxed?
After assessment, you can decide what is best to do next with your day.

How can I make this day amazing?
Action!

Write these questions down and leave them next to your bed to remind yourself for the first few mornings.

> **"** Success isn't always about greatness.
> It's about consistency. Consistent
> hard work gains success. Greatness will come. **"**
>
> ~ **Dwayne Johnson**

Set your alarm

If you use your phone as your alarm clock then set it with a reminder, such as 'time to read'! Maybe reading isn't the first item or habit on your morning agenda, but it's worth a try to get you into a better morning routine. Don't hit the snooze button. Remind yourself that those unconscious minutes could be put to better use!

Breathe!

Take a moment to notice your breathing. Slow it down and inhale deeper and feel the benefits after a minute or two. Yoga helps to bring awareness to your breath and a good morning stretch really limbers you up for the day. Try this instead of a run, or alternate activities daily.

> **"** No one can get inner peace by pouncing on it. **"**
>
> ~ **Harry Emerson Fosdick**

Meditate

Feel more peaceful and centred by including meditation in your morning routine. You could even do this in bed before getting up! If you are new to meditation, there are plenty of guided meditation apps available.

"The thing about meditation is: you become more and more you."

~ David Lynch

Your phone

Except from checking the time and switching off your alarm – wait until later to check your emails, messages, the news, or social media. Choose to get out of bed more gracefully. You can absorb all this information later on; once you're thriving.

"Every morning you have the choice to continue sleeping with your dreams or get up to chase them."

~ Carmelo Anthony

Wake up to a clean room!
Which means tidy it before you get into bed at night! Don't leave your clothes lying around on the floor. Create a space which feels more peaceful and welcoming, and you will notice a new energy surrounds you when you rise. Plus, it's one less thing to do this morning so you have time for beneficial actions.

"Sometimes cleaning our rooms will clean our minds too."
~ Unknown

Get active
Some people find this harder than others. You don't have to commit to a 10k run every morning, but you can build your fitness level up slowly. Everyone must start somewhere! Weight loss is a popular goal, and maintaining a healthy weight is good for longevity, so why not get it out of the way before heading to work? Take the opportunity for some 'me' time if you can work out whilst the rest of the house is sleeping.

"I don't run to add days to my life, I run to add life to my days."
~ Ronald Rook

Connect with your pet Get breakfast together, take them for a walk, and play before heading off to work. Feel happier and start the day on a joyful note. Don't have a pet? Why not? It's nearly impossible to be angry or sad after playing with a cute animal.

> **"If I could be half the person my dog is, I'd be twice the human I am. "**
>
> **~ Charles Yu**

Track your habits

There are plenty of apps available to help you tick off each morning activity. You may prefer an acclaimed morning routine or customise the app with your own morning tasks. Alternatively, you could use a chalk board or a notepad. The importance of habit tracking is to watch your growth and see the correlation with your desired results. When you look back at your records, you will have a true vision of your progress and see if it's working or not. You can log your habits in a journal.

> **"Without reflection, we can make excuses, create rationalisations, and lie to ourselves. We have no process for determining whether we are performing better or worse compared to yesterday. "**
>
> **~ James Clear**

Write in your journal

Improve your writing skills and set your intentions each morning. Journals are not just for reflecting on memories or events but recognising your overall development. Write about your ideas, emotions, and experiences. Describe your problems and how you overcome them. Explain what you are grateful for and don't worry about repeating yourself from page to page. This is how you stay on track.

Plan a weekly, monthly, quarterly, and annual check in. Try using mantras to focus on your intentions. It doesn't need to take more than five minutes of journaling to create a salubrious space where you express yourself freely.

" *Journaling is like whispering to one's self and listening at the same time.* "

~ Mina Murray

There are plenty of planners and diaries on the market, but an empty notepad will suffice. Use this basic tool to establish your future goals and accomplish them by identifying a bulletproof course of action. Determine what problems you need to solve in your day to day life and confront them. Journals are like therapists, sharing your thoughts and feelings without judgement or interruption. Your journal is a safe place where you can write down your worries. This can be cathartic and free up space in your mind.

Revisit your journals to boost your spirit and accomplish future endeavours.

" Take up one idea. Make that one idea your life - think of it, dream of it, live on that idea. Let the brain, muscles, nerves, every part of your body, be full of that idea, and just leave every other idea alone. This is the way to success. "

~ Swami Vivekananda

Finding The Right Quotes For You

" If your goal sets you apart
from the crowd, stay alone. **"**

~ **Unknown**

Wherever you find a quote which resonates with you, and you'll find them anywhere, it's about recruiting them to manifest positive change in your behaviour.

❝ Employ your time in improving yourself by other men's writings, so that you shall gain easily what others have laboured hard for. ❞

~ Socrates

<u>Check out *Rise & Thrive*:</u>

Quotes To Start Your Day on social media.

@riseandthrivequotes

Convince Yourself

" *The question you should be asking isn't,* '*What do I want?*' *or* '*What are my goals?*' *but* '*What would excite me?*"

~ Timothy Ferriss

Nothing good ever came easy, right? And you're here for change! While some changes come easier than others, some changes require a more active approach to shift your mind. You can train your brain - like training your muscles in the gym! – and when you master this training, your mind and spirit become immensely powerful.

Want to make a change? Then repeat positive benefits to yourself like a mantra. Want to lose weight? But on the way to work you can't avoid walking past the bakery which triggers your sugar craving? Convince yourself that cupcakes are not tasty (which they obviously are!) because then you won't be tempted to eat them and put weight on! 'It's just sugar, it'll leave me craving all day' or 'I won't feel good about eating it later'.

Repeat what works for you to ingrain it in your mind.

Convince yourself that you will feel so proud when you get up an hour earlier tomorrow and accomplish more than you did yesterday.

Convince yourself that you will feel so much better and more energetic after exercising this morning, so that you condition yourself to work out regularly.

See where this is going? Keep doing all these tasks which you KNOW are good for you and prove to yourself that you're right! (That cupcake will always be tasty though...)

Forget what everyone else is doing – or not doing. Try to better yourself and see how it makes you feel. You will have a newfound confidence that won't go unnoticed by 'everyone else'. Don't do it FOR anyone else, because whatever you're trying to achieve simply won't stick.

The point here, in convincing yourself, is to commit to make the time for your personal development. Your positivity. Others who are not making time for their personal development won't grow and see results like you will!

Achieve

"Optimism is the faith that leads to achievement. Nothing can be done without hope and confidence. **"**

~ Helen Keller

You're here reading this book for a reason. You want to elevate your mindset in one way or another. It's important to remember the best way to do this is by taking lots of small steps towards your end goal. These are called 'micro improvements' if each day is better than the last. If we slip up? Hey! It's ok - we're human. We just reset and try again. We can always try again! It is the small steps of progress that are imperceptible until the results finally show in massive exhibition.

Each day you can improve a tiny bit and these daily actions are going to compound. So, think about a topic where you want to excel. Ask yourself why you want to progress in this chosen area and how you are slowly going to achieve success. Repeat these lines during your morning walk, run or workout!

Begin the first line with 'each day I can...'

Try applying this, 'each day I can' method to your area of progress!

Fitness

Each day I can:
Go a little harder
Stretch a little further
Move a little faster

Life

Each day I can:
Love a little harder
Laugh a little more
Let go a little easier

Investing

Each day I can:
Save a little extra
Spend a little less
Compound a little more

Too Much?

" *Character cannot be developed in ease and quiet. Only through experience of **trial** and **suffering** can the soul be strengthened, ambition inspired, and success achieved.* "

~ Helen Keller

All these ideas might seem like you need a whole day to carry out your morning! But these tips don't have to take very long and your life is worthy of investing in with this essential time for progression.

These tips advise you to cut OUT some of your current morning habits (such as TV, checking your emails, or social media) to prepare you for your morning the night before. Set your alarm clock earlier than normal to give your new morning a chance.

You're more likely to create a habit if it's there in front of you. The night before, leave your journal and *Rise & Thrive* book next to the kettle, on the dining table, or wherever you choose to carry out your morning routine. By making it visual, you are more likely to remember!

Before committing to your new morning routine, take these suggested activities for a test drive to see which ones best suit your lifestyle and personality! You may surprise yourself...

**❝ *When we get to the end of the story,
you will know more than you do now...* ❞**

~ Hans Christian Andersen

Sharing

" Keep your fears to yourself
but share your courage with others. **"**

~ Robert Louis Stevenson

...is caring. Why don't you spread the positivity and share some of these quotes with your loved ones? Or at your morning work meeting? Help others to thrive throughout their day. Create a support network which will in turn encourage you as a group to thrive.

"We can't help everyone,
but everyone can help someone."

~ Ronald Reagan

Success

" **Success is not final,
failure is not fatal:
it is the courage
to continue that counts.** "

~ Winston Churchill

Ask yourself - NOW – 'what am I trying to achieve?' Today, tomorrow, this year or later in life. Usually, you're trying to achieve a few things simultaneously. Financial freedom, happy homelife, a new skill... Write them down and spend some time reflecting on each of your goals.

" It is our attitude at the beginning of a difficult task which, more than anything else, will affect its successful outcome. "

~ William James

"You must do the things you think you cannot do."

~ Eleanor Roosevelt

Are you achieving your goals and at what rate? If you are, fantastic! Keep it up! If you feel that you're falling flat on your face, then don't get frustrated. There are lots of techniques out there. Journaling, for one, really helps to track your progress. Give it a bash, along with these quotes to manifest successful behaviour.

**"If I cannot do great things,
I can do small things in a great way."**

~ Martin Luther King Jr.

" You've got to say, I think that if I keep working at this and want it badly enough I can have it. It's called perseverance. "

~ Lee Iacocca

If we believe in our ability to achieve, then our mindset is going to work wonders throughout the day. This perspective is not only motivating but it's positive. We're determined to keep that uplifting energy from dawn until dusk so that we succeed.

" The great accomplishments of man have resulted from the transmission of ideas of enthusiasm. "

~ Thomas J. Watson

Good Morning!

" The secret to a good morning
is to watch the sunrise with an open heart. "

~ Anthony T. Hincks

Smile! Even if you want to dive back under the covers and return to your dreams. Smiling tricks your brain into feelings of happiness, so make sure you are wearing yours now and get ready for your morning read.

" *How sweet the morning air is! See how that one little cloud floats like a pink feather from some gigantic flamingo. Now the red rim of the sun pushes itself over the London cloud-bank. It shines on a good many folk, but on none, I dare bet, who are on a stranger errand than you and I. How small we feel with our petty ambitions and strivings in the presence of the great elemental forces of Nature!* "

~ Arthur Conan Doyle

It's a new day! You might have already smashed some goals before opening this book - like your morning meditation, workout, or journaling. Before that cup of coffee, make sure you drink a glass of water first thing in the morning to rehydrate and kickstart your organs. You're going to need their cooperation in order to tackle the day.

" *There's always a story. It's all stories, really.*
The sun coming up every day is a story.
Everything's got a story in it.
Change the story, change the world. **"**

~ Terry Pratchett

**" Rise above the storm,
and you will find the sunshine. "**

~ Mario Fernandez

" Life. This morning the sun made me adore it.
It had, behind the dripping pine trees,
the oriental brightness, orange and crimson,
of a living being, a rose and an apple,
in the physical and ideal fusion of
a true and daily paradise. "

~ Juan Ramón Jiménez

You're going to have approximately 60,000 thoughts today. That sounds gruelling, right? Well let's try and channel those thoughts to be as optimistic and driven as possible.

Set those intentions into motion and have a great day!

" MAKE EACH DAY YOUR MASTERPIECE. "

~ John Wooden

"It's time to start living the life you've imagined."

~ Henry James

" I remind myself every morning:
Nothing I say this day will teach me anything.
So, if I'm going to learn, I must do it by listening. **"**

~ **Larry King**

Gratitude

" *You can't have everything...*
where would you put it? "

~ Steven Wright

"Start each day with a grateful heart."
~ Roy Bennett

Ahhh, the quality of being thankful.

When you're experiencing gratitude, you're also feeling other positive emotions which helps to deal with adversity and improves your mental well-being, giving you the adroitness to create stronger relationships with others. Think about it, if you focus on feeling grateful and you're generally more optimistic because of it, isn't this going to motivate you to achieve those personal goals you've been setting for yourself? If you're aggravated and pessimistic, then you're hardly going to be in the mood to break a sweat, eat healthily, spend time with loved ones, or put extra time into your work or business.

The word gratitude is derived from the Latin word 'gratia', which means grace, graciousness, or gratefulness. With a gratitude attitude you acknowledge the goodness in life! Gratitude is closely linked with happiness (and who doesn't want to be happy?). This source of happiness may be accessible outside of yourself. Gratitude can also help people connect to something larger than themselves as individuals, within their community, surrounding nature, or religion.

" The primary cause of unhappiness is never the situation, but rather your thoughts about the situation. "

~ Eckhart Tolle

Gratitude is the readiness to show appreciation for something and to return kindness. Wouldn't the world be a better place if we were all more grateful for what we already have? Sometimes, we wrongly focus on what we don't have and what we want, instead of being thankful for possessing all that we need.

" Very little is needed to make a happy life; it is all within yourself, in your way of thinking. "

~ Marcus Aurelius

Read cheerful quotes about gratitude to find your way to positivity and happiness. A little perspective goes a long way to elevate your outlook for the day.

"When asked if my cup is half-full or half-empty, my only response is that I am thankful I have a cup. "

~ Sam Lefkowitz

Having A Bad Day?

❝ Everything will be okay in the end.
If it's not okay, it's not the end. **❞**

~ John Lennon

Ok, you have woken up on the wrong side of the bed this morning and things are not going your way. Or maybe yesterday didn't go as planned. Well today is a new day, so you're NOT going to let negativity affect you. Easier said than done, of course.

" When you reach the end of your rope, tie a knot in it and hang on. **"**

~ Thomas Jefferson

Remember the tip about smiling to trick your brain into thinking you're happy? If that fails, read these quotes to reset, adjust your perspective, and smash the day ahead.

" *It is never too late to be what you might have been.* **"**

~ **George Eliot**

" It's never too late to start over.
If you weren't happy with yesterday,
try something different today.
Don't stay stuck, do better. **"**

~ Alex Elle

" A champion is defined not
by their wins but by how
they can recover when they fall. "

~ Serena Williams

" A life spent making mistakes is not only more honorable, but more useful than a life spent doing nothing. "

~ George Bernard Shaw

"The most difficult times for many of us are the ones we give ourselves."

~ Pema Chödrön

" You are only one decision away
from a totally different life. **"**

~ Mark Batterson

You got this! Take a breath, reflect on what you have, all you have achieved, feel grateful and recognise your worth. Then we can start solving your problems and tell this bad day where to shove it.

Rise & Thrive is here to save the day!

" Breathe. Let go.
And remind yourself that
this very moment is the only
one you know you have for sure. **"**

~ Oprah Winfrey

"REMEMBER, IF YOU EVER
NEED A HELPING HAND,
IT'S AT THE END OF YOUR ARM."

~Audrey Hepburn

Inspiration

" YOU ARE NOT
IN THE UNIVERSE,
YOU ARE THE UNIVERSE. "

~ Eckhart Tolle

We could all benefit from a little inspiration here and there, right? A 'pick me up' between the peaks and troughs of life. Inspiration is equally important to boost a low mood, enhance a good mood, or awaken a neutral mood. Try the quotes in this inspirational section to get you going today. Embrace a positive mindset.

"My mission in life is not merely to survive, but to thrive. "

~ Maya Angelou

"I alone cannot change the world,
but I can cast a stone across
the water to create many ripples. **"**

~ Mother Teresa

" *I've missed more than*
9,000 shots in my career.
I've lost almost 300 games.
26 times I've been trusted
to take the game winning shot
and missed. I've failed over
and over and over again in my life.
And that is why I succeed. „

~ Micheal Jordan

" Life is too short to be small. **"**

~ **Timothy Ferriss**

"The two most important days in your life are the day you are born and the day you find out why."

~ **Mark Twain**

Eleanor Roosevelt is remembered as one of America's finest First Ladies. She is admired for her confidence, fearlessness, and true kindness. Eleanor organised women-only conferences in the White House, to give female journalists a voice. By cause and effect, this led the papers to hire more women reporters.

As an advocate for equality, she defied the segregation laws. By sitting in the middle of the segregation during a conference, she sent a bold message for racial justice – as they were highly unlikely to arrest the President's wife!

When Eleanor was a delegate of the United Nation, she assisted in drafting the declaration of human rights. Having a feminist on the list of composers means women all over the world have her influence to be appreciative of.

Eleanor's life's work has encouraged many women and there are, thankfully, plentiful quotes recorded of her wise words so she lives on to inspire.

" To handle yourself, use your head;
to handle others, use your heart. "

~ Eleanor Roosevelt

" Great minds discuss ideas; average minds
discuss events; small minds discuss people. "

~ Eleanor Roosevelt

" No one can make you feel
inferior without your consent. "

~ Eleanor Roosevelt

Self Worth

" The only person you should try to be better than,
is the person you were yesterday. **"**

~ Matty Mullins

This book is all about improving your mornings, to upgrade your mindset throughout the day, which will continuously enhance your LIFE! So, it's only right that we take time to honour ourselves and our worth.

**"I have too many flaws to be perfect.
But I have too many blessings
to be ungrateful. "**

~ Zig Ziglar

It can be difficult to find your place in the world. No one has all the answers and nobody walking the earth is perfect. We try with all our might to progress, so sometimes we need to have a look in the rear-view mirror of life to register how far we've come.

We rehearse our answer to the anticipated interview question: *"Where do you see yourself in five years?"* But how often do you look back five years from where you are with the same question?

" Focus on how far you've come... not how far you have to go. "

~ Rick Warren

Take a moment to reflect on how far you have come. Have you ever consciously registered the goals you've triumphed or the significant progress you have accomplished? What a great way to feel more positive by taking inspiration from OURSELVES!

**❝ I am not what happened to me.
I am what I choose to become. ❞**

~ Carl Gustav Jung

During your developmental phase, it's important not be too hard on yourself. You have days where you need to push outside your comfort zone, but not every single day.

Life can get a bit much sometimes and when this happens, you need to take a break and adjust your morning accordingly.

Try reading over these quotes on those heavier days to maintain the cognitive growth you're hoping to achieve and the positive mindset you intend to gain.

"If only you could sense how important you are to the lives of those you meet; how important you can be to people you may never even dream of. There is something of yourself that you leave at every meeting with another person. "

~ Fred Rogers

"To be yourself in a world that
is constantly trying to make you something
else is the greatest accomplishment. "

~ **Ralph Waldo Emerson**

Enjoy The Rest Of Your Day

" From today onwards, take complete control of your life. Decide, once and for all, to be the master of your fate. Run your own race. Discover your calling and you will start to experience the ecstasy of an inspired life. "

~ Robin S. Sharma

Thank you for reading this book and keep up the good work! You managed to find the time in your mornings to make *Rise & Thrive* a part of your day. Stick with your new habit and healthy morning routine to maintain your positive mindset. When you're thriving, you will earn the reward for it later in the day.

> " Keep putting out good.
> It will come back to you
> tenfold in unexpected ways. "
> ~ **Farrah Gray**

Each morning you've worked your way through quotes on achieving, practising gratitude, discovering inspiration, realising your self-worth, and many other tools for holistic motivation. Hopefully, you found quotes which will continue to help you put your life into perspective, switch on your positive mental attitude, and enable you to channel your personal growth. Carry these lines of wisdom with you which have resonated inside your heart.

The quotes may have given you some new ideas to implement. Get right to it! The reading time in the morning should have reduced any stress and activated your brain so keep reading and the ideas should keep flowing.

Continue to convince yourself to become wiser and healthier. Be mindful of those little white lies. Often, the hardest person to persuade is ourselves. 'I am a morning person' – I hear you say!

Don't look for self-validation from others, find it within. It's there, promise! You read this book for you. When you rise out of bed, you have created a routine for yourself, not for anybody else. Keep those mornings sacred so you can thrive. When you thrive, you'll see that it's contagious and your family, friends, and colleagues will all benefit from your motivational mood.

" *Sometimes the people around you won't understand your journey. They don't need to. It's not for them.* **"**
~ **Joubert Botha**

Remember that when you aren't thriving in the morning, it is your responsibility to do something about it. Make slight tweaks to get your motivation rebooted. Don't settle for an ordinary life. Thrive! Wake up with a desire to improve and help others in your life. Maintain your sleep routine to compliment your mornings so you wake up with that desire.

If your schedule was showing results and has suddenly stopped... identify the trigger and reset. Find out the reason why the results have shifted. Is it your diet? If you normally skip breakfast, try skipping lunch or dinner instead. Is it your job? If you work from home, try changing your hours or scheduling your breaks at different times. Is it your exercise regime? If you normally workout first thing, try an evening workout or attempt a different kind of exercise – for example, throw some bedtime yoga in!

" *Variety's the very spice of life,*
that gives it all its flavour. "

~ William Cowper

Can't get enough quotes?

- Check out *Rise & Thrive*: Quotes To Start Your Day on social media **@riseandthrivequotes**

- Write quotes on sticky notes and place them next to your bed to read when you first wake up

- Save a new one to your phone or desktop background

- Send your favourites to friends and family or anyone who you think might need that quote in their life right now

- Tape them to your mirror

- Carry them around in your wallet

- Continuously repeat them in your mind until they stick

- Share quotes and words of wisdom with *Rise & Thrive* on social media!

- Your self-improvement doesn't end with this book.

- One last quote before you go...

" Don't wait for change. You change. **"**

~ Earl Nightingale

Acknowledgements

"Employ your time in improving yourself
by other men's writings, so that you shall
gain easily what others have labored hard for. **"**

~ Socrates

Thank you to my husband-to-be, Doug, for believing in me. He always supports my crazy ideas and because of him, I was urged to share my morning quotes with the (scary) big, wide world. I am so lucky to be marrying the smartest man I've ever met. His reassurance and encouragement for my dream has never faltered.

Thank you to my family, especially my mother, Anne, who is a fellow early bird. She proofread *Rise & Thrive* not once, not twice, but three times! My sister, Charlotte, has influenced many of the creative decisions for *Rise & Thrive* with her eye for style and attention to what's trending.

Thank you to my work colleagues, especially Jazmin and Jerome, who helped turn my idea into a book and checked up on my progress along the way.

Thank you to all my amazing friends and cousins who spurred me on throughout the process and gave me so many great ideas as the book was evolving. I owe a special thanks to the Connelly family for their boundless, sounding board.

I started writing this book when I was in lockdown, so I have used 'The Great Pause' productively. However, the Corona virus pandemic caused sadness and strain for me and my family. I must thank all the medical staff who have worked tirelessly and the key workers who kept the world spinning. These brave people didn't have the opportunity to use this time because they were fighting for us at the front line. I appreciate the immense courage to face the risks, especially in the beginning when there was so much uncertainty. I saw the time as an opportunity to write a book, but I wish the world had never been subject to the widespread effects of COVID-19 and the damage left in its wake. It has been a stressful and worrisome time for everyone.

I am grateful to the journalists, influencers, and companies who share inspiring quotes on various platforms, which I continue to use in my daily ritual.

Lastly, and most importantly, I must acknowledge all the wise people in the world who have blessed us, over hundreds of years, with such profound words to apply in our day-to-day lives. May we educate and shape young minds so that they provide us with another generation of wise and wonderful quotes.

DISCLAIMER

"The problem with quotes found on the internet is that they are often not true.„

~ Abraham Lincoln

That quote from Lincoln is obviously a joke. The main thing you should take away from this book is that regardless of WHO said the quote, you can thrive today, tomorrow, the day after, and next week! Hopefully, these quotes assist in shaping your day with positive, healthy vibes. Shake off any morning grouchiness and start your day in a happy mood. You don't have to be sparkling like a Disney princess, but you don't need to hiss at the sun either. Enjoy the book and be open to the change it encourages.

" THE GREATEST MISTAKE A MAN CAN MAKE IS TO BE AFRAID OF MAKING ONE. "

~ Elbert Hubbard

Made in the USA
Middletown, DE
04 April 2022